garden

structure

garden
structures

USING SHAPE TO TRANSFORM YOUR GARDEN

JENNY HENDY

LORENZ BOOKS

This edition is published by Lorenz Books

Lorenz Books is an imprint of Anness Publishing Ltd
Hermes House, 88–89 Blackfriars Road, London SE1 8HA
tel. 020 7401 2077; fax 020 7633 9499
www.lorenzbooks.com; info@anness.com

© Anness Publishing Ltd 2003

UK agent: The Manning Partnership Ltd, 6 The Old Dairy,
Melcombe Road, Bath BA2 3LR; tel. 01225 478444; fax
01225 478440; sales@manning-partnership.co.uk

UK distributor: Grantham Book Services Ltd,
Isaac Newton Way, Alma Park Industrial Estate, Grantham,
Lincs NG31 9SD; tel. 01476 541080; fax 01476 541061;
orders@gbs.tbs-ltd.co.uk

North American agent/distributor: National Book
Network, 4501 Forbes Boulevard, Suite 200, Lanham,
MD 20706; tel. 301 459 3366; fax 301 429 5746;
www.nbnbooks.com

Australian agent/distributor: Pan Macmillan Australia,
Level 18, St Martins Tower, 31 Market St, Sydney,
NSW 2000; tel. 1300 135 113; fax 1300 135 103;
customer.service@macmillan.com.au

New Zealand agent/distributor: David Bateman Ltd,
30 Tarndale Grove, Off Bush Road, Albany, Auckland;
tel. (09) 415 7664; fax (09) 415 8892

A CIP catalogue record for this book is available from
the British Library.

Publisher: Joanna Lorenz
Managing Editor: Judith Simons
Senior Editor: Sarah Ainley
Designer: Louise Clements
Indexer: Helen Snaith
Production Controller: Stephen Lang

1 2 3 4 5 6 7 8 9 10

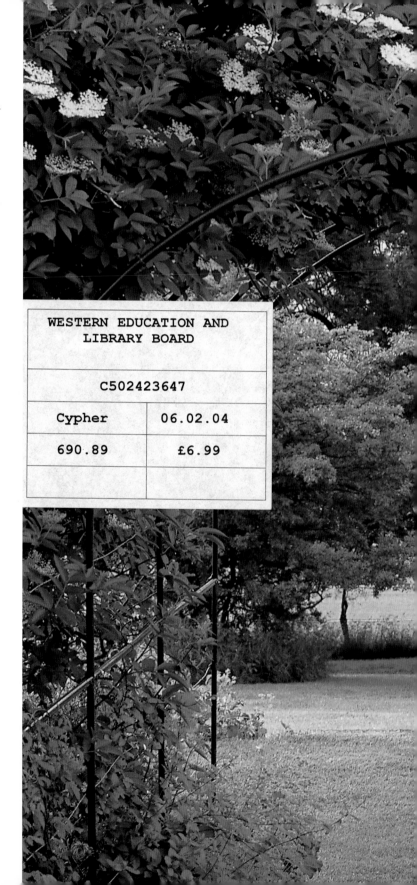

contents

introduction

Ornamental buildings and decorative structures, such as archways, can be built to enhance views from the house or to create wonderful vistas as you make your way round the garden. Structures such as conservatories and pergolas can add extra "rooms" to a garden, in the form of sheltered seating or areas for dining. They can be hidden away or camouflaged to create an intimate space for adults or children and a spark of excitement for anyone who discovers their whereabouts.

Outdoor constructions often have a theatrical element and there are all kinds of design tricks and decorative techniques to enhance their dramatic impact. Illusion is a key factor and this is borne out when you come across a folly designed to look like an ancient classical temple but which is in fact a façade or piece of clever fakery, without so much as a stone pillar or carved inscription in sight.

Beautifully designed garden buildings are seen in formal landscape gardens and in the laid out grounds of historic mansion houses. These are wonderful places for inspiration but difficult to recreate when your backyard is the size of a postage stamp. But there is really nothing to stop you from adding an element of grandeur to your own little piece of heaven. Whether you prefer rustic simplicity, urban chic or old-fashioned elegance, this book includes a host of ideas to suit your taste and budget.

In very small garden plots it can be quite a challenge to incorporate structures like a playhouse for the children or an arbour for grown-ups. This is where good integrated design and planting comes in – something that you will find plenty of advice about in the following pages. Garden structures, especially those that incorporate seating or create the atmosphere of an outdoor room, encourage us to spend more time outdoors with friends and family – eating, drinking or simply relaxing alfresco. What better reason to start building?

ABOVE: *A visit to an architectural salvage yard can unearth all manner of stonework and statuary, which if strategically placed is capable of adding a touch of grandeur to even a relatively modest garden space.*

RIGHT: *This large Gothic window frame creates a dramatic focal point. Placing grand or familiar structures in unusual situations introduces a surreal element that lightens the mood and creates an atmosphere of fun and anticipation.*

Research, planning and sorting out the practicalities are essential parts of the process of siting large, ornamental garden structures.

If you've always dreamed of a summerhouse then you will want the end result to live up to expectations and it would be foolish to rush into things. Think everything through from start to finish. As well as choosing a design, you will need to decide where to place the structure for best effect, and consider landscaping requirements. Are you hoping to use the building at night and will it need lighting anyway, so that it can be seen from the house? What colour would you like the structure to be and how might you give it a more imaginative look? Would you make more use of an existing building if you gave it a makeover? This chapter will help you make these decisions.

preliminaries

a sense of place

If you are thinking of adding a decorative building or structure to the garden, it is vital that you work on the proposed location before you go shopping, otherwise it may not even fit the intended space.

Even though it is sometimes possible to customize the shape and size of a garden structure, especially when the component parts come as separate modules, if you buy off the peg you need to be confident that the structure or building will be in proportion to the house and the surrounding garden. This is particularly important if it is to be used as a focal point.

To help you visualize how an architectural feature will look in its setting, it is a good idea to take a variety of photographs of the site and then sketch the structure on to the print with a black marker pen. You could try out a range of options to see which style or design works best. A large building could be overpowering in a small plot and, equally, a small structure might end up looking insignificant and lost in a spacious garden. It might seem like a lot of work at the time, but it really does pay to erect a simple mock-up of the building or structure using bamboo stakes lashed together to form a skeletal outline. You can then walk around or through this 3-D model and get a really good feel for how the final structure will look and work out practically. Making adjustments to the model is far less costly than altering or rebuilding what is likely to be quite an expensive purchase.

Buildings should always look as though they are well anchored within the garden landscape, and not adrift within the space. Finding a way to tie the feature in to the garden's basic structure is the key to making this happen; skilful planting can also help to blend the stark lines of a building in to its surroundings. In an informal layout, one corner of the plot may provide a ready-made site for a summerhouse, because of the "protection" offered by the fencing or hedging behind. Another technique involves setting the building within its own formal garden.

LEFT: *Here, the curving grass pathway leads the eye subtly towards an ornamental structure partly hidden by the surrounding trees and shrubs. Man-made elements usually stand out clearly against a natural garden backdrop.*

ABOVE: *This delightful little sentry box is the main element of a clever stage set that utilizes symmetry and formality to great effect. The beds and pathways are mirror images and the twinned, round-headed silver weeping pear trees give a sense of depth and proportion to the scene.*

Some knowledge of perspective and vanishing points can be useful in setting up the position for a decorative building. Paths are a good way to observe how perspective manipulates our view of the garden. Even one that meanders off into the distance and is here and there obscured by planting will eventually lead the eye to an end point. And something positioned there will automatically become the focus of attention. Water also draws the eye, and a building set next to a pool, especially when its image is reflected in the mirror-like surface, is enhanced beyond measure.

In a formal setting, whether period or contemporary, there is ample opportunity to make a dramatic statement with a building or pergola. Here you can utilize the strong geometric lines of the ground plan (formed by paving, lawns, clipped hedging and so on) to direct the eye towards the structure in question. Where garden "rooms" have a symmetrical design, especially when surrounded by walls of trellis or hedging, it is relatively easy to make a theatrical set piece using a decorative building, such as an arbour, as the main focus. You could, for example, use a central pathway or long narrow lily pool to lead the eye from the viewpoint to the arbour. Another way to fashion a setting for a building is to use the space in the foreground, creating a pattern, such as a knot garden, parterre, formal potager or pebble mosaic, to act as window dressing.

A simpler device for emphasizing the importance of the building is to plant an avenue that leads directly towards it. This could be anything from topiary pieces set either side of a pathway, to pleached lime trees or a vine covered pergola. Doorways and entrances can also be strengthened visually by using a matching pair of architectural plants as "sentinels".

Garden structures do not have to be situated at the end of a plot or against a wall. Along a major axis you could construct a number of decorative features, such as a gazebo with simple bench seats or a rose-covered archway, pergola or walkway. At each of these punctuation points your eye should be held for a moment by the construction itself, as well as by decorative detailing designed to enhance the effect: a circular paving feature, a garden ornament or a fountain. Set up the next focal point some way ahead to encourage further exploration.

LEFT: *A thatched arbour could be the perfect place to relax and enjoy the sights and scents of the garden, but it is usually necessary to feel that a sitting area is private and secluded before you can truly relax.*

ABOVE: *Unusual in its design, this curving metal structure needs to be placed in the right spot for its shape to be properly appreciated. High clipped beech hedges and a straight brick path make a strong contrast and help to focus the eye towards the terracotta urns beneath the tree.*

materials

Regardless of design, what you use to build your garden structure can have a profound effect on the final appearance. It also helps if you match new constructions with existing elements.

Traditional materials, especially those with a weathered or organic quality, are very popular for garden structures. This is partly because many constructions are designed with a period feel, and it is usually the case that the older something looks the more easily it blends into the garden landscape.

Achieving this aged look is more straightforward now that manufacturers are producing building materials with an antique finish. It can also be worth visiting architectural salvage yards to pick up reclaimed items, including roof and floor tiles, old timbers, window frames and doors.

Straw thatch is a traditional roofing material for garden buildings, but if you can't find a thatcher operating in your area, you could buy modular thatching units via mail order. An alternative for an old-style building might be to use wooden shingles, clay pantiles or copper sheeting. At one time your woodworking skills had to be pretty good to cut out ornate gingerbread bargeboarding, but now with power tools, like the jigsaw, and suitable materials, notably marine quality plywood, you can make almost anything provided you have a template. Always wear a face mask when cutting wood.

Modern designs can still make use of classic materials but the range of products available now means that you can create avant garde constructions that sit very comfortably in a contemporary setting. Walls of galvanized wire gauze let in the light but provide shelter from the wind; they make an interesting substitute for wooden trelliswork and are beautiful at night if lit with coloured floodlights. Glass bricks have also become available in recent years and these are ideal for making light airy structures, especially associated with water. Meanwhile, shiny metal sheeting, made from chrome or stainless steel, will reflect the surrounding greenery, creating a surreal effect. But modern design is often about using everyday materials in imaginative ways.

TOP: *The materials of this wattle shelter blend perfectly with the wild garden surrounds.*

ABOVE: *A simple bridge made from wooden planks.*

RIGHT: *To create an authentic Mediterranean courtyard garden, the walls were rendered and treated to a soft terracotta colour wash. Large rustic clay tiles finish off the roof and wall.*

practicalities

It is always a good idea to check with your local council or estate office whether you need planning permission to build, even if the structure is only temporary, since there may be restrictions in place.

It is important to remember that, being fairly large, garden buildings may impact negatively on your neighbours' outlook, and towers and other structures that allow you to see over the boundary could have an effect on someone else's privacy. For the sake of harmony, it may be wise to consult with neighbours about your project before you begin work.

Wooden buildings, such as sheds and summerhouses, need a waterproof base to prevent moisture being absorbed from the soil. Wood is naturally very durable provided it is allowed to dry out thoroughly between showers, and having a flow of air beneath a building is one way to ensure this. You can build bases in the form of a concrete slab laid over hardcore, paving slabs or breeze blocks, but rather than laying the building directly on top, it is best to rest it on joists, such as concrete or tanalised wooden posts laid along the ground to distribute the weight. Another solution is for the building to be brick-built part of the way up, with a waterproof membrane inserted two bricks above path level. Keep plants and long grasses away from the base of wooden buildings, since they can trap moisture and prevent airflow. A surround of gravel, pebbles or paving also helps to prevent soil splash.

Softwood posts, such as those supporting a wooden arbour, archway or pergola, are best fitted into metal sockets for easy replacement. They can be set directly into holes filled with concrete, but even if the wood is tanalised, the base may start to rot within ten years. Securing posts in metal sockets, which keep the base just above ground level, extends the life of the wood and makes it easier to replace the posts at a later date.

Providing electricity in the building opens up possibilities with regard to lighting and power supply. Use armoured ducting to carry the cabling from the main junction box and run it beneath pathways to lessen the risk of damage. If you are in any doubt about wiring call in a qualified electrician.

ABOVE: *When planning a conservatory, pick a design that is in keeping with the surroundings. Avoid hot sunny walls as this may make it impossible to maintain a pleasant temperature range, and don't forget to check whether you need planning permission.*

RIGHT: *Proper foundations for wooden buildings, as well as adequate guttering and drainage, help to keep the structure dry. This rustic water feature needs adjusting as water is splashing back on to the timber and it may eventually rot.*

makeovers

One way to inject an element of style into your garden is to carry out a makeover on the existing structures, such as sheds and other outbuildings. Sometimes just a few cosmetic touches are enough.

Your chosen project could be to make an existing feature into the central focus of a themed garden, such as a Roman villa, Japanese tea garden or colonial trading post in the jungle.

Simply applying a fresh coat of paint or coloured wood stain can work a minor miracle on a lacklustre building or tired-looking garden structure, such as a pergola, and of course paint is relatively cheap to play around with. Certain colour schemes strongly suggest particular geographic or imaginary locations. For example a zingy combination of lime green and watermelon pink would be ideal for a Caribbean beach shack, while shades of purple, maroon and cardinal red might be used to conjure up a land of magic and mysticism. On metalwork, you could reproduce weathering effects like copper verdigris to artificially age the structure, and adding a touch of gold leaf would suggest either opulence or, if you were going for a "distressed" look, faded elegance.

Some kind of pattern, motif or, suggesting a link with antiquity, letters and symbols like hieroglyphics or Roman numerals, could also be applied to a building's façade. On a blue-walled Wendy house you might hand-paint giant sunflowers or favourite characters from a children's storybook, or to satisfy a teenager's urge to escape from the house you could turn an old shed into a den by applying camouflage.

LEFT: *Beneath this decorative rendering is a simple breeze block construction. Before the cement is dry, it is relatively easy to apply relief patterns, including ceramic, shell or pebble mosaics, or to insert stone plaques and carved panels to conjure up an atmosphere of rustic antiquity.*

RIGHT: *This old kitchen chair helps to set the scene along with other props that create the feel of a tumbledown fisherman's shelter. The colours also contribute to the illusion, as would appropriate planting.*

Simple trompe-l'oeil techniques can be used to suggest 3-D elements, such as classical columns and carved stonework – you don't even have to be naturally artistic since stencil templates are available. False windows or door apertures can also be painted in to relieve a monotonous stretch of wall, and these are even more effective if real-life shutters or an old door are nailed in place. If your ability allows, you could even paint in a lifelike mural, such as a cat sitting on a windowsill.

Another way to create illusion is to apply some kind of façade, such as cement rendering with a mosaic or shell decoration, perhaps, or an imprinted pattern to mimic blocks of dressed stone. On a wooden building, such as an enchanted cottage in the woods, you could nail or glue on "organic" texturing, such as pine cones, pieces of cork bark, driftwood or even hand-woven panels of withies. Heather cladding, which comes in rolls, is easy to fix in place using a heavy-duty staple gun, and it can transform a standard garden shed into a rustic retreat. Meanwhile, split bamboo gives an unmistakable flavour of the East and is very easy to apply.

For a more imaginative alternative to roofing felt, try wooden shingles, old clay tiles or reclaimed slates, which are perfect for a period setting because they already have that sought-after weathered look. Meanwhile, long straw thatching can be applied to create follies as various as a Polynesian hut, a *Wind in the Willows* boathouse or a fairy-tale cottage.

Once you have done the basic work on a building, the next stage is to introduce some props and to consider the surrounding landscaping, including plants, hedges and screens as well as paving. For a beachcomber's paradise, evidence of makeshift mending with frayed twine or rough planks of wood would make the scene more convincing. Then you could dress the stage with coloured glass fishermen's floats, nets and traditional creels filled with pebbles and shells. Build a wooden boardwalk from reclaimed wood over a shingle "beach" and plant blue-grey tussock-forming grasses to suggest salt marsh and dune grass. Alternatively, props for a colonial trading post in tropical Asia might include bamboo-filled Eastern glazed jars with a dragon motif, wind chimes and stone reproduction temple dogs.

TOP: *A Wendy house can be so much more appealing to children if it is painted in bright colours and made to feel like part of the grown-ups' garden.*

LEFT: *The plain, whitewashed wall of a country cottage has been given a farmhouse flavour using a collection of old-fashioned containers and tools.*

ABOVE: *For an Eastern look, use split bamboo roll to clad fences and to reroof garden structures and buildings, such as outhouses and sheds. Enhance the effect by mimicking red lacquer, painting the wooden uprights and bargeboards with bright red gloss paint.*

colourways

There is no doubt that colour is one of the chief factors affecting our view of the environment, influencing us on an emotional level and suggesting associations with other countries and cultures.

Too much of one man-made colour can be overwhelming, especially if it is particularly eye-catching, and in the garden, where nature exerts the greater influence, bold colours are best used as an occasional accent.

When deciding what shade to paint the woodwork, metalwork or rendering of a building or structure, you need to take a variety of other factors into consideration. For example, if you were establishing a period feel for the garden, you might choose more muted shades. Most paint manufacturers include a range of these historically accurate colours that take their inspiration from some of the great mansion houses – creams, greys, sage and willow greens, classic blues and a wide range of earth tones.

Another point to bear in mind is climate or, more specifically, quality of light. In a hot, sunny, dry region, where clear blue skies are an everyday occurrence, the light is much stronger and purer than it is in, say, a northern maritime region, where the light is frequently filtered by cloud and rain. In clear light, stronger, more vivid colours – hot reds and oranges and strident mustard yellows – positively glow, whereas beneath filtered light these shades can look flat and harsh. In this case you are safe with almost any shade of blue as well as soft clear yellow, deeper reds and maroon.

TOP LEFT: *Bright colours bring sunshine and a holiday atmosphere into the garden. On wood, use weatherproof paints and stains; on metal, use exterior gloss.*

LEFT: *Rich earthy reds blend easily with planting and make a change from the usual timber colours.*

RIGHT: *Tone fabrics with paints and stains to give a softer, more co-ordinated feel to arbours and other garden buildings.*

When it comes to painting the exterior walls of the house, many of us prefer to be conventional and stick to neutral colours and those that are commonly used in the neighbourhood. But the great thing about having a garden with an element of seclusion is that you usually have more freedom to do as you please and can have fun experimenting. After all, if you don't like the finished effect, you can always start again and paint over your handiwork. In a large garden, particularly one partitioned off into separate areas, you can afford to be quite daring and original. In a small plot, where structures are closer to the house, the space will feel larger if the colour schemes are unified and more muted.

Traditionally, wooden structures, such as fences and sheds, were given an annual coating of dark brown creosote and the colours of wood stain that came along later were limited to a few browns and the occasional green. Fortunately, in recent years, there has been a veritable explosion of coloured exterior paints and stains, and you can now have textured masonry paint made up in the colour of your choice.

Wooden buildings and structures made from decorative treillage tend to offer more possibilities for creative paintwork. For example, you could use contrasting colours to pick out the architectural detail – doors and windows, shutters and architraving, or paint the posts and the framework around trellis infills in a darker shade.

Rendering a brick or breeze block building also makes it easier to introduce colour. You might apply a terracotta colour wash to a rough stucco finish within a Mediterranean-style garden, or a deep purple to a building in a modern minimalist setting – it will tone beautifully with galvanized metal, raw wood and cobbles. Clear lemon yellow also has a contemporary feel and would help to lift an area planted with an abundance of dark evergreens.

Try to match your colour scheme to the mood or style you wish to create. Gentle blues and soft grey-greens work well on structures within a romantic country or cottage garden setting, enhancing pastel flower borders and these shades are perhaps preferable to the traditional pure white, which can be harsh and difficult to maintain.

TOP: *Vivid lime green makes a Caribbean-style backdrop to these bright red geraniums. When painting the garden, consider what colour plants are likely to be in the vicinity.*

LEFT: *Painted in the same shades of blue and lilac, all the elements in this scene flow together beautifully, from the picket fence to the pergola.*

ABOVE: *This grey-blue is a smart, period colour that makes an excellent foil for the dark green topiary pictured. It also works well with buff-coloured natural stone and gravel, or with silver and white plantings in a romantic setting, helping to engender an atmosphere of timelessness.*

lighting

By day, a decorative structure might be a subtle but pleasing focal point, but at night, with adventurous lighting, there could be an amazing transformation – like having two garden features instead of one.

Hidden lighting can give very atmospheric results. Putting a light behind a fascia board in the apex of a wooden arbour to gently illuminate the interior will make the arbour seem so much more welcoming. Tiny white outdoor fairy lights add a touch of magic for night-time dining and can be woven through the foliage of an overhanging tree or flowers on a pergola. Fairy lights could also be used to create a romantic ambience in a more formal garden, twinkling through the trelliswork of a pavilion or in the branches of a pleached lime avenue.

Mini halogen floodlights set at ground level to highlight a building from the base can produce real drama and you can use different colours to create or enhance a particular mood or atmosphere. Focused light coming from one direction creates well-defined shadows, accentuating the form and texture of architectural features. Mini spotlights and uplighters may be used to highlight specific features, such as ornate masonry, but you will need to play around with the angle and position to achieve the best results before securing them in place.

You can choose lighting to suit the specific style of building or structure. If you wanted to light up a boathouse folly you could use nautical style bulkhead lamps or hang a storm lantern in the doorway. Or to lead the way to a Japanese teahouse, you might set candles into traditional stone lanterns. Generally speaking though, most light fitments should be well camouflaged, even recessed into walls, paving or decking.

Don't forget the safety advantages of lighting. Illuminating pathways, pools and changes in level makes walking around the garden at night a much less risky proposition. Think about having infrared sensors fitted so that the outdoor lighting circuit comes on at dusk. If you have difficulty getting mains electricity to the site, consider solar-powered lamps, which now have rechargeable batteries and a reasonable output.

TOP LEFT: *Take advantage of pergola crossbeams and hang lanterns to illuminate the terrace below. You can also use simple night lights along the top walls or, for a touch of elegance, introduce some tall outdoor candelabra.*

BOTTOM LEFT: *You can sit outside long into the night once you have some lighting. This highly decorative candelabrum takes centre stage, but you could also provide some soft background lighting by placing a small electric light to shine down on the veranda.*

ABOVE: *Recessed lighting subtly illuminates these columns and the central walkway, creating a stylish outdoor room that can be used at any time, day or night.*

camouflage

One of the ways to maintain suspense in the garden is by concealing certain areas and allowing the scene to gradually unfold. Garden structures often seem better integrated when they are half hidden.

The ground plan of the garden – the layout of the borders, pathways and lawns – tends to dictate where a structure is to be sited, but even when it is technically in the right place, it can still look very new and somewhat stark. You can help a building or structure be more quickly absorbed into the body of the garden through appropriate landscaping. For example, you might integrate a cottage-style building by surrounding it with a riot of country flowers and roses and even a low picket fence. Planting also helps to soften the hard architectural lines and strengthens the illusion that a building has been there for years. The use of one or two mature specimen plants, such as topiary pieces or climbers trained over large obelisks, lends an air of maturity to the site. However, bear in mind that plants grow and if you don't select with care, you might end up obscuring the feature that is the principal attraction.

In contrast to the subtle "dressing" of structures with climbers, shrubbery and herbs, there is the opposite situation where you want to completely obliterate the building, or at least blur the outline so that instead of seeing the eyesore you just see glimpses of wall together with the doors and windows. A building such as a large concrete shed with a corrugated iron roof presents you with a dilemma because the building, though far from decorative, provides useful storage. In this case, the best strategy may be to smother the roof and walls with quick-growing, even rampageous climbers. Ones offering speedy cover as well as flowers include Russian vine (*Fallopia baldschuanicum*), *Clematis montana* 'Elizabeth', the evergreen honeysuckle (*Lonicera japonica* 'Halliana'), rambler roses like 'Bobbie James' and common jasmine (*Jasminum officinale*). Ivy (*Hedera*) and climbing hydrangea (*Hydrangea anomala subsp. petiolaris*) both of which are ideal for shady aspects, take two or three years to start climbing in earnest, but then they suddenly take off so don't give up on them.

LEFT: *Part of the roofline of this garden structure has been left exposed because of its decorative effect, even though the object of the planting is to create seclusion.*

ABOVE: *Use rustic screens made from collected stems and twigs to camouflage unsightly buildings.*

TOP: *Inexpensive frameworks can be covered with surprising speed, using fast-growing climbers and shrubs, to create secret bowers. An overhanging tree canopy can be used instead if you do not have anything sufficiently mature in the garden.*

The following pages amount to a celebration of garden buildings and structures that are both practical and aesthetically pleasing.

Buildings and structures can enhance not only the appearance but also the ambience of our outdoor world. Even the humble shed has a role, its standing in the garden assured. Once the potting shed was as much architecture as the average suburban gardener aspired to, but in recent years garden centres and do-it-yourself stores have become ever more adventurous, responding to the demand generated by popular television gardening shows and glamorous magazine features.

A huge variety of constructions are now available from arbours to Wendy houses and the wide range of styles means that you are sure to find something to suit your budget and personal taste. Meanwhile, modern-day follies foster our need for escapism when we are looking for somewhere to take time out from the pressures of everyday living.

structures

decorative buildings

Ever since man first began creating gardens for pleasure, architecture has been a vital component.
Sometimes it functions merely as a pleasing backdrop but it can also make a bold theatrical statement.

Decorative buildings should enhance the aesthetic qualities of the garden, with their graceful lines and proportions, and introduce colour and ornament to lift the landscape during the winter months. Garden buildings can also play a role in making the garden feel more intimate and adding a frisson of excitement. They can be places where one could imagine secret assignations or romantic trysts taking place. Even the more reserved amongst us will acknowledge that they can help to engender a relaxed, even playful atmosphere.

There is something magical about being out in a garden retreat, far enough away from the house to forget about worldly cares for a short while. Gardens provide wonderful opportunities for escapism and a decorative building, such as a summerhouse, pavilion or gazebo can play a key role in feeding your imagination, allowing you the freedom to relax and unwind in comfort.

When it comes to selecting a building you may find the choice at garden centres is limited to mainly period-style reproductions made from wood. These can be expensive to buy and standards can vary between suppliers. It certainly pays to shop around. Check out adverts in home and garden magazines and search the internet for specialists. If you buy by mail order, ask to see an example to check the build quality.

LEFT: *You are unlikely to find a building as quirky as this off the peg. If you want something out of the ordinary, think about customizing an existing structure with decorative additions or specify an unusual roofline, window or door detailing. And don't forget the power of colour.*

RIGHT: *Decorative stone or brick-built garden buildings can help to create an atmosphere of calm and permanence. Even if you can't afford something as grand as this beautiful old summerhouse, a rendered building made from inexpensive breeze blocks may still be an option.*

Over the centuries, all kinds of buildings have been designed to enhance enjoyment of the garden and some types still have links to a particular era or geographical location.

The summerhouse is strongly associated with Victorian romanticism, and with its abundance of glass it is a place to retire from the chill breeze of an otherwise sunny day, or seek shelter during a summer shower. In the summerhouse you can relax with all of the basic comforts, read a book or take afternoon tea with friends. A pavilion is a decorative building with open or partially screened sides in which to sit and contemplate your surroundings in style. A Chinese pavilion would traditionally have been built over a lake or pool, appearing to float on the water's edge. In contrast, the Italian-style loggia may be a simple, rustic building with a rude, pantile or thatched roof and natural stone walls or a roughly rendered façade. It looks like a long open shelter extending from a building, and is ideal for dining alfresco. The gazebo takes many forms and was traditionally a place to take in the view, which is why it is often raised up or placed somewhere with a panoramic outlook. It may be square, hexagonal or octagonal in design, is usually small and enclosed, with doors that open out on to a particular vista.

LEFT: *An Italian-style loggia provides shelter and plenty of space, and it is a perfect place for outdoor dining.*

ABOVE FROM LEFT: *Gothic archways give this building an air of antiquity. A romantic arbour of wrought iron stands in the middle of a wildflower meadow.*

The roofline of a garden building can be one of the most appealing elements. Sometimes a mere glimpse of a gable end or a decorative finial draws us on to explore. Other architectural details, such as steps, decks and verandas, unusually shaped windows and shutters or a quirky doorway, add greatly to the look and feel of a building.

If you are reasonably confident of your do-it-yourself skills, and are seeking to introduce an original touch, you may choose to construct to your own design. Certainly, given the right environment, a rustic, handmade quality can be part of a building's charm. You can also customize an off-the-peg timber building relatively easily and a few cosmetic changes could transform and elevate even a modestly priced piece of garden architecture. Constructions in stone, rendered breeze blocks or brick should, however, be left to the experts and will probably require some planning permission.

The word summerhouse conjures an image of colonial elegance, an all-weather home-from-home.

arbours and bowers

These are amongst the easiest of all decorative structures to accommodate in the garden and having such wonderfully romantic overtones, they are also highly desirable.

Arbours first started out as airy structures covered in climbers, under which you could stand or sit, bathed in dappled light, enjoying the profusion of flowers. They reached a height of popularity in the 18th and 19th centuries, when highly ornate wooden treillage and metalwork designs became fashionable. During the Regency period in particular, ravishing Moorish temples and birdcages of filigree wirework decorated the gardens of the wealthy. You can still buy this sort of structure, and they look heavenly smothered in a rambling rose.

But arbours can be built on much more modest lines, and today we tend to think of an arbour in terms of a covered bench seat, most often made from timber and trellis panels, which creates a sense of seclusion and refuge. You can buy a reasonably wide range of wooden or wirework arbours in kit form with styles ranging from gothic to rustic. More formal designs are perfect for creating a definitive focal point at the end of a vista, for example, completing a long straight path lined with lavender hedging or a pergola walkway. Another method of making an arbour is to clip a bench-size alcove into an existing hedge or shrub border and to allow the sides and top to grow out so that the alcove becomes even more recessed over time.

The bower is a variation of the arbour and as a sitting place is far more wild and secretive, created as it is from an interweaving of scented shrubs and climbers. The bower is a lovely feature for a relaxed country or cottage garden, occupying a secluded corner. You can provide the basic structure for a bower from trellis panels, rustic poles or from a wirework arch attached to a wall or fence to give it the necessary rigidity. Plant around the base with quick-growing fragrant shrubs like mock orange and shrub roses as well as evergreens, such as Mexican orange blossom, and cover the sides and top with perfumed climbers.

TOP LEFT: *Set back in a trellis alcove, this pretty arbour would be ideal for a small courtyard garden, with a collection of pots and hanging baskets providing an abundance of flowers and foliage.*

BOTTOM LEFT: *Secret bowers can be constructed using pergola-like structures which are then festooned with flowers for late spring and summer, including deliciously fragrant climbers.*

RIGHT: *A rusting iron-framed bower smothered in climbers is perfect for a relaxed country garden or to provide seating in an old apple orchard.*

pergolas

A pergola is an overhead structure that either provides a pleasant leafy walkway along a garden path or the "ceiling" for an outdoor garden room, with dappled shade for sitting out or dining alfresco.

A pergola can be freestanding or attached to a wall, and the sides may be left open or filled with trellis panels. Pergolas are almost invariably covered with climbers, and the fragrance that accumulates beneath the structure on a still summer day can be quite intoxicating. Some climbers, such as wisteria, are especially effective. Not only do they have the vigour required to cover the large structure, but their long pendulous and fragrant blooms also hang down through the struts at just above head height.

Walkways have the effect of leading the eye and focusing it on the end point and this fact mustn't be ignored if you and your garden visitors are not to feel cheated. Always make sure there is some reward in store – perhaps a bench seat from which you can look back through the tunnel of greenery, or a large ornamental pot or statue.

Pergolas and walkways can be constructed from timber, from large metal hoops or from a combination of stone or brick pillars with deep wooden crosspieces. All-wooden modular pergolas can now be purchased flat-packed from garden centres and do-it-yourself stores. Be sure to buy only hardwood, tanalized or naturally rot-resistant timber. The pieces are pre-cut so that they slot into one another and it is relatively straightforward to erect a modest-sized pergola over a weekend. If you can't find a ready-made structure to suit, local timber yards may be willing to cut the pieces for you. Brick or stone pillars are a more costly proposition and may demand the services of a skilled bricklayer.

Whatever type of pergola you choose, plan its construction and design very carefully. The most common mistake people make is to get the proportions wrong. In particular, ensure that you have sufficient head height, allowing for the growth of climbers. Anything less than about 8ft (2.5m) of free space will feel cramped and claustrophobic.

LEFT: *Certain plants, such as wisteria and* Laburnum *'Vossii', are particularly suited to planting over pergola walkways, allowing their long flowing tresses to hang down through the struts.*

RIGHT: *A heavy wooden-framed pergola attached to the house wall can create the atmosphere of an outdoor room, ideal for dining.*

BELOW: *Arches of apple trees create an informal and productive walkway in this country garden. A feeling of intimacy is maintained by keeping the pathway narrow and encouraging a froth of geraniums to tumble over the edges.*

glass houses

Some of the most elegant garden buildings are made from glass. Glass structures always feel light, having a network of narrow supports in the form of wood or metal and, often, ornate rooflines.

Glass provides shelter from the wind and, being transparent, a glass building can create the ideal conditions for growing subtropical and Mediterranean plant species. But this may also create problems. When ultraviolet light passes through the walls of a conservatory or greenhouse, the energy is absorbed, converted into infrared and radiated back into the air in the form of heat. Without proper ventilation this heat builds up and the temperature can easily get high enough to damage plant growth as well as making it uncomfortable for humans.

One of the biggest problems with the design of glass buildings today is lack of ventilation. Roof vents are essential since hot air rises but you also need vents in the walls to allow air to be drawn in from outside. If there is an option for extra vents at the time of purchase, take it, and if possible fit automatic vent openers. Interior blinds will lessen the glare but do not cut out heat. To keep the interior cool use external roll-down blinds made from split bamboo cane or apply white greenhouse shade wash. Aspect is also important. If you want to avoid baking on a sunny day, site your conservatory on an east- or north-facing wall, never south or west.

LEFT: *Glass and water share properties of transparency and reflection. This domed shelter is so light and airy that it doesn't in any way impede the views across the water. Even the platform that it is set on appears to be afloat. When furnishing a glass building it is vital to avoid anything too solid. Wicker, bamboo and wrought iron are ideal.*

TOP RIGHT: *One way to help a working greenhouse blend into the garden is to paint the framework in a dark shade, such as bottle green.*

RIGHT: *This period inspired glass house design with open sides is acting like an airy summerhouse within the garden and is at once practical and highly ornamental.*

The attractive architectural styling of a well-made conservatory can add greatly to the appearance and value of a property. Nowadays, having a conservatory built is often a way of acquiring extra living space to use year round. Sealed double-glazed units reduce heat loss at night and through the winter, and the central heating system can often be extended from the house to maintain a comfortable temperature. In northern temperate zones, the therapeutic benefits of a light, airy living space in winter cannot be overlooked. Unfortunately plants can often suffer in the dry atmosphere, and if you want to create a green oasis, compromises must be made. The need for relatively high humidity means that carpets are best replaced by tiles so that the floor can be damped down, and furniture needs to be moisture-resistant.

If the only wall available for a conservatory is south or west facing, the best choice of glass house would be a sun room that has a solid roof, with or without skylights, and partially bricked walls. Paint the interior white or a pale, light reflecting shade and you will still have many of the benefits of a conservatory without the problems of overheating.

Practical greenhouses come in all shapes and sizes from rectangular to octagonal but remember that it may be more difficult to obtain accessories to fit unusually shaped houses.

LEFT: The Palladian roofline and impressive stepped entranceway to this contemporary glass building give it a powerful presence.

ABOVE FROM LEFT: Hide the contents of your greenhouse with foreground planting. A hobby greenhouse, used for raising flowering and foliage plants, can be made even more ornamental if the framework is painted.

Enthusiasts can also buy specialist greenhouses for growing alpines, orchids and so on. It is important to decide what you are going to use the house for and to work out how much bench space you require before purchase.

Most greenhouses are aluminium framed but some of the more expensive designs have wooden glazing bars. Wooden framed greenhouses blend in well with the garden but eventually weathering and warping can lead to loose panes.

One of the problems with greenhouses from an aesthetic standpoint is that you can see right through and the interior may be quite unsightly. The roofline could be a feature, however, and camouflage planting that hides the sides may be called for. In the vegetable garden this might be something as simple as runner beans trained on a framework of bamboo canes. A flower or mixed shrub border is another option or even a hedge clipped waist high.

Sitting in a glass house building can feel almost like being outside in the garden, especially if the garden is lit.

versatile sheds

The ubiquitous garden shed has potential far beyond being a mere repository for lawnmowers, garden tools, toys and assorted junk. In fact, a garden shed can become a secret hideaway.

Children and adults alike are drawn to garden dens and in this pressured, hi-tech world of ours there is something very appealing about decamping to a rustic idyll surrounded by plants and wildlife that is far enough away from the house for you not to be able to hear the phone.

A well-used potting shed can look remarkably attractive in an earthy, organic sense, with the mellow wooden walls hung with garden tools and paraphernalia for raising seedlings and young plants piled up on the potting bench. Even during autumn and winter there can be visual treats when the harvest of fruits and vegetables is in storage – individually wrapped apples, pears and quinces laid out in boxes; brightly coloured squashes and pumpkins; and onions and garlic tied in bunches.

Places like this have a comfortable, old-fashioned feel and though they are no doubt acting as a hub for garden activities it is not surprising that you often find home-from-home touches too. Having an electricity supply makes a big difference to the comfort levels. You can power a kettle to make a hot drink, put a light on at night and run a heater in cold weather. After all, you may start sowing and pricking out seedlings in the early spring, when ground frosts and cold temperatures are still very likely.

LEFT: *A stone or brick-built shed, garage or workshop can be incorporated into the garden by dressing the walls with hanging pots and planters, or by growing self-clinging plants like ivy and climbing hydrangea. Applying painted trellis panels to the shed walls is another useful softening technique.*

RIGHT: *Smothering the garden shed with rambler roses and other vigorous climbers, such as jasmine, softens the hard lines and helps the building become absorbed into the garden. The results are often quite cottagey and rustic, especially when a softly coloured wood stain is used.*

In the surrounds of a traditional garden shed you might find such things as trays of plants waiting to be transferred to the garden; a large rainwater butt; bundles of long bamboo canes and perhaps home grown fertilizer in the form of barrels of fermenting comfrey or nettle liquor. A wise gardener would also add a simple bench seat – somewhere to sit on a warm sunny day and take a well-earned break from their chores.

A shed located in the garden doesn't necessarily have to be connected with garden maintenance. By fitting sheets of thermal insulation in the walls and roof, carpet and underlay, a power supply and possibly a telephone extension, sheds can quite easily be converted into extra rooms for use year round. In fact for a relatively small outlay you could have an office space, a studio or workshop, a playroom for the children or a hobby room for adults. You can buy wooden sheds in all manner of shapes and sizes and suppliers will often offer a delivery and construction service. All you have to do is to build a suitable base and this can be a simple matter of laying down hardcore and concrete joists to raise the structure off the ground slightly, thereby preventing rotting.

Garden sheds make ideal workspaces for people involved in creative activities – artists, craftsmen, writers and designers. Being surrounded by nature can provide that all-important spark of inspiration. Make the route from the house, the area around the doorway and views from the windows as pleasant as possible and if you can, obscure any glimpses of the house or road to prevent distraction. You might want to cocoon the building with foliage and flowers, drawing it deeper into the garden, but remember to leave a space for sitting outside and relaxing. A raised veranda or deck could blend in perfectly.

LEFT: *This large garden shed is well sited, forming as it does an attractive backdrop to the brick-paved potager. Use screens of climbing vegetables, such as beans and squashes, mingled with climbing nasturtiums or sweet peas to obtain a little privacy.*

TOP RIGHT: *If you are going for a rustic or cottage garden look, decorate the area around the shed with a range of utilitarian garden props.*

RIGHT: *Inside this potting shed is a veritable Aladdin's cave, a fascinating mixture of garden paraphernalia.*

follies

Follies are fantasy buildings and constructions that help to influence mood and atmosphere.
They became fashionable in the 17th century, and there was a strong resurgence in the 1800s.

Originally follies were designed with frequent references to classical myths and legends, though humour and touches of surrealism crept in too. Follies have always engendered a romantic air of escapism but nowadays you don't have to look to the Gothic novel for your inspiration. Plans for a folly could come from your favourite dream landscape and may be quite futuristic. Some of the best examples have an element of quirkiness about them, perhaps where the designer has placed a fairly ordinary object in an extraordinary way, such as a stone fireplace, apparently freestanding and overgrown with rambling climbers.

One of the fun aspects of building a folly is theatrical deception. Skilful placing and camouflaging with creepers means that you can get away with an image as grand as a Greek temple, but which is actually nothing more than a façade. A painted silhouette or cut-out of sheet metal or marine plywood may be all that is needed to convince the onlooker that the architectural feature at the bottom of the garden is a solid 3-D construction. And even in a period landscape, there is no need to spend a fortune on a building. The Victorians discovered that a crumbling ruin or a few fragments of masonry emerging from the ground was enough to create mystery and intrigue. Encouraging mosses, lichens and ivy to colonize stonework, or using proprietary aging compounds to take away the sheen of newness, works wonders for generating a look of antiquity. It also helps to site objects in forgotten corners amongst long grasses and wildflowers.

Visit architectural salvage yards for broken pillars, blocks of dressed stone and fragments of sculpture and create an ancient relic of your own. Even something like a large, ornate window frame could be used to suggest the remains of a grand house. You can also incorporate elements bought from garden centres, such as stone Buddhas or reproduction gargoyles.

LEFT: *Like the gates of a lost temple in some far distant land, this clever trompe l'oeil is a magnificent piece of theatre. Notice how the mirrors and a tangle of climbers help to carry off the illusion.*

ABOVE: *This quirky dovecote is straight out of a fairytale land. Follies such as this can often be made by elaborating on existing structures or by sculpting or manipulating mature plantings.*

With modern building materials and a little imagination you can create all kinds of fantasy constructions. For example, concrete mixed with plasticizer can be sculpted into smooth, curving shapes with surprising ease. Apply over a base of breeze blocks covered with a moulding of wire mesh to confer structural integrity and to achieve the basic form you are looking for. You can texture the surface before it dries, using a wetted nylon hand brush and other tools. You can also apply decorations: pebbles, coloured glass beads, shells, ceramic "fossil" ammonites and so on. In a cool shady spot, textured concrete is rapidly colonized by algae, helping it to merge in to the surrounding greenery. Ornamental stone and concrete elements such as lions-head wall masks and other pieces of statuary can also be incorporated into do-it-yourself structures – the mortar helping to disguise the joins – or combined to create an imposing façade around a doorway or garden mirror.

Follies made from items that have ceased to be useful in terms of their original purpose are ideal for experimenting. You could, for example, take an old leaky rowing boat and part fill it with shingle and ornamental grasses to form the focus of a fisherman's retreat. Continuing in that vein, you might turn a tiny outdoor storeroom into a brightly coloured bathing hut. In fact any existing shed or outbuilding has the potential for conversion into a folly of some kind, whether it be a boathouse, a fairytale cottage, or a jungle hut.

For an illusion to be moderately convincing though, you really need to set the stage and add the necessary props and "scenery". Signposts can be fun for children of all ages. Use them to point the way along an adventure trail, perhaps leading to a hidden temple, deep in the South American jungle. Access could be via a rickety rope bridge with a narrow dirt track, partially obscured by giant grasses, bamboos and other lush, tropical-looking foliage. For a more grown-up theme, build a Chinese pavilion next to a large, naturalistic pool complete with stepping-stones and moss-covered rocks.

RIGHT: *Follies often have dual roles, being in some way practical as well as beautiful or thought provoking. This thatched Japanese teahouse could be used for dining but the interior need not be Eastern in style.*

arches

If you were asked to picture a view of a romantic garden, an archway festooned with fragrant roses and honeysuckle would almost certainly be one of the elements that would spring to mind.

There is something deliciously sensual about having flowers at head height that you can examine with ease, revelling in the perfume. But arches don't just offer decorative support for climbers, they sometimes have symbolic meaning and certainly they have a design function. Passing beneath an archway usually signifies that you are moving from one area to another, ideally to a part of the garden with a distinctly different character, and with a little theatrical stage setting this can evoke a frisson of excitement and anticipation.

Arches may be square topped, curved or pointed and they may be made from timber and trellis, metal, stone or clipped hedging. However, the key to success has less to do with construction materials and more to do with integrating the archway into the fabric of the garden. Archways are most commonly erected over a pathway for practical purposes, but they should never be left standing high and dry or they will look awkward and out of place. It is best to have quite substantial plantings on either side, with a combination of tall plants and others that taper away to ground level. An even more successful method of cementing an archway into the overall structure of the garden is to flank it with a hedge, or to use trellis panelling covered with climbers, or a foreground planting of shrubs. This focuses the view through the arch, and allows you to frame a decorative element such as a piece of sculpture much more effectively.

When planting an arch, ensure that the structure is firmly supported as it could become top heavy with foliage and vulnerable to being blown over. Choose your climbers with care and avoid very vigorous specimens like rambler roses and *Clematis montana*. Instead go for the dainty, early-flowering cultivars, such as those derived from *Clematis alpina* and *C. macropetala*; summer and autumn flowering viticella types and the spectacular large-flowered hybrids.

LEFT: *Dappled shade and the luminous green of backlit foliage created by a climber-clad walkway provide pleasing contrasts of atmosphere, especially in an area with little relief from sunlight.*

RIGHT: *It would seem that this is the entrance to a particularly important area of the garden. In fact, the steps and pathway may lead nowhere in particular but the image created is still very convincing.*

BELOW: *This Gothic arch has a remarkably elegant line and it would be a shame to completely smother it with climbers. Instead, use annual flowering climbers or several of the less vigorous clematises to provide flowers from late spring into autumn.*

bridges

The gentle arc of an Eastern-style bridge is very pleasing to the eye and can act as a serene focal point within a naturalistic garden setting. It doesn't even matter if there is water present.

As with archways, bridges sometimes symbolise a crossing over to another place or even an imaginary realm, and you could introduce an air of mystery and romance by creating a special island retreat, either surrounded by water or by a dry moat, accessible only via a bridge.

In a Chinese-style water garden, a bridge might be painted lacquer red with gold detailing to really catch the eye. By contrast, a bridge set in a wild or woodland garden would need to have a more earthy, organic look, made from reclaimed timber, heavy, roughly worked stone, or from rustic poles, with a simple handrail. Under the shade of the trees, the structure would soon become colonized with algae and it could be slippery in wet weather, so it is a good idea to cover the base with chicken wire for extra grip.

Constructing a bridge or walkway across a large pool can be a tricky proposition and one for which you might need professional help. Safety is of paramount importance. Foundation piers of rot-resistant timber may need to be sunk deep into the mud before the rest of the structure can be attached. To build a bridge across a pond lined with butyl rubber, build breeze block piers, cushioning the liner first to prevent puncture. To span a relatively narrow stream, you simply need to lay a couple of heavy beams across the gap and then nail down boarding for a walkway.

TOP LEFT: *Create the illusion of a stream in your garden by setting a bridge across a narrow pool, using cobbles to simulate a stream bed and plants to camouflage the edges.*

LEFT: *Lacquer red is strongly associated with Eastern gardens.*

RIGHT: *This staggered arrangement of large stepping-stones is a traditional pattern in Japanese water gardens, but natural stone arranged in random fashion always works well in a naturalistic setting. Set the piers on soft cushioning fabric to prevent the bricks from puncturing the liner.*

living structures

The great advantage of using plants to create structure in the garden is that you can build large elements for relatively little outlay – you simply have to adopt a more patient attitude to the process.

You can literally clip a hedge or a shrub into the green equivalent of bricks and mortar or dressed stone. Plants are "plastic" or malleable, and provided you choose the right species for the task at hand, you can create almost any shape you desire: columns, pyramids, domes, and so on.

Why not try clipping your hedge into traditional castellations or avant garde waves, or reach flights of fancy with stylized birds? Not only can "rooms" be built with walls of foliage, but you could also clip buttresses and create arches or grand doorways with classically inspired finials. On a smaller scale you could simply carve out a niche to display a vase or statue on a plinth. If a maze is too large for your plot, consider a scaled down version – a parterre or knot garden – or simply contain the exuberant plantings of your borders with low clipped green walls. Even in the depths of winter, the garden will still have a wonderful 3-D structure.

On a less formal theme you can mould the plants in a mature garden to enhance their natural form – billowing clouds, for example, or hollow out an overgrown shrubbery to create a lovers' bower or a den for the kids. Alternatively, try your hand at willow sculpture, using live willow whips, planted and then woven together to build an arching canopy.

LEFT: *Eccentric, larger-than-life shapes cut from yew make interesting partners for the spiky cordylines. The plants could have been clipped into columns or pyramids. Yew, or in warmer climes,* Podocarpus, *grows surprisingly quickly but if you want something in half the time, try structures grown from* Thuja plicata.

RIGHT: *Topiary is often referred to as green architecture and in this case it is clearly mimicking some kind of formal stone construction. You can also shape living walls to create unusual seating areas. Always use a plant that will regenerate if it is cut back hard.*

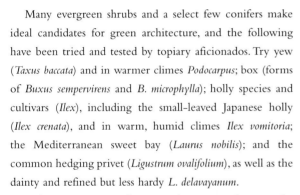

Many evergreen shrubs and a select few conifers make ideal candidates for green architecture, and the following have been tried and tested by topiary aficionados. Try yew (*Taxus baccata*) and in warmer climes *Podocarpus*; box (forms of *Buxus sempervirens* and *B. microphylla*); holly species and cultivars (*Ilex*), including the small-leaved Japanese holly (*Ilex crenata*), and in warm, humid climes *Ilex vomitoria*; the Mediterranean sweet bay (*Laurus nobilis*); and the common hedging privet (*Ligustrum ovalifolium*), as well as the dainty and refined but less hardy *L. delavayanum*.

A key requirement for a good topiary subject is the ability to regrow when cut back hard into old wood – with long-term projects you will eventually need to reshape and possibly rejuvenate your structures in this way. Yew is one of the few conifers that has this ability, but if you train a plant regularly from the beginning, you can even use fast-growing hedging conifers such as the infamous Leyland cypress, or the more easily controlled Western red cedar (*Thuja plicata*).

Small-leaved plants, such as yew and box, can be clipped with shears to create smooth forms that have a similar quality to chiselled stone. Larger-leaved subjects, such as bay

LEFT: *An avenue of mop-headed* Robinia *is pleasing in its simplicity. Even in winter, the bare stems provide structure.*

ABOVE FROM LEFT: *Planting compartments can be made from clipped box, which also provides evergreen structure and pattern out of the flowering season. Box can be clipped into organic forms, creating undulating landscapes.*

and holly are ideally shaped with secateurs to avoid unsightly half-cut leaves, but most people resort to shears or even powered hedge trimmers for larger projects.

A number of deciduous trees and shrubs also have great potential for creating big formal structures, such as avenues and walkways. These include beech and hornbeam, both of which hang on to their coppery coloured autumn leaves through the winter, and forms of lime (*Tilia*), a favourite for pleaching – a type of training where the canopy is thinned out, selecting certain young, pliable branches which are then attached to a horizontal framework. Since the tree is growing in a flat plane, it takes up far less room and so you could even afford to plant a double row of trees to line a pathway. The effect is rather like a hedge raised up on stilts.

Clipped or trained to geometrical perfection, plants can be transformed into green architecture – living bricks and mortar.

tents and awnings

Temporary fabric structures are great fun to set up during the summer months, especially for garden parties, and you can really let your imagination run riot with their design.

There are plenty of benefits to having a temporary structure, such as a tent, not least because you can easily dismantle it at the end of the summer or when you want to create a different effect in your garden.

The temporary nature of tents also means you are more likely to experiment with more radical ideas. For example, you could create an Arabian Nights-style shelter, the interior of which could be draped with luxurious fabric remnants, the floor covered with rugs and cushions. Candle lanterns would create a magical atmosphere at night, and during the day the light passing through fabric is soft and diffuse, creating a soothing environment for relaxed lounging.

Children will play for hours in a Native American-style tepee, which can be easily constructed using a tripod of rustic poles lashed together at the top and draped with canvas. You might also take inspiration from Arthurian legend, creating a striped pavilion with a fluttering pennant.

For an adult level of sophistication, there are metal-framed mini marquees of square or hexagonal construction, normally roofed with cream or deep green canvas, and these are handy for summer barbecues and dining alfresco, especially where the climate is less than reliable. Again, you can dress up these basic constructions by pinning on translucent muslin drapes, fresh flower garlands and ribbons for special occasions. Such structures are best erected in a relatively sheltered spot, however, as they may take off in a freak gust.

Just as a climber-clad pergola can create the atmosphere of an outdoor room, so too can a canvas awning. Nowadays there are many variations on the standard rectangular shelter that slopes down from the house wall. Awnings made from coloured canvas and other modern weatherproof materials may be sculpted to form pleasing sail-like canopies that curve and sometimes overlap.

LEFT: *Canvas awnings made from brightly coloured cloth can really help to set the right mood for outdoor dining and are not difficult to arrange. You can utilize pergolas, covering the framework with inexpensive remnants.*

ABOVE: *Looking like something from the Arabian Nights tales, this luxurious pavilion, complete with drapes and floor cushions, is set up for a summer party. The front panels can be rolled down for extra shade.*

child's play

It is sometimes difficult to entice children away from the television and into the fresh air outdoors, but most will love to have their own place in the garden beyond the jurisdiction of their parents.

The treehouse has always been a favourite, capturing the imagination of children and adults alike. These can vary from a simple platform of planks to a timber building complete with trap door and rope ladder. The main drawback is likely to be not having a tree large enough or sturdy enough to provide a solid framework. The answer is to create extra support in the form of wooden pillars or metal scaffolding poles set firmly into the ground, or to build a tower-like structure to replace the tree. The ramshackle construction of the typical treehouse is part of the attraction for children and you can use all manner of reclaimed wood. The matter of key importance here is safety, and you should check the structure on a regular basis.

A rugged timber climbing frame with rope nets, ladders, ramps, slides, swings, aerial walkways or rope bridges would present fantastic opportunities for adventure play. The frame could grow with the size of the children, and you can purchase ready-made climbing frames in modular units to fit the space available. Frames constructed largely of timber will blend into the garden easily, especially when built in a woodland or wild landscape. Active older children love to climb, and if you don't have room in your garden for something extensive, you could simply construct a watchtower, complete with flagpole from which to fly a pirate's flag.

Younger children are generally happy to play in a traditional Wendy house, but these can be very expensive to purchase ready-made. When choosing a design it is a good idea to check that your children will have sufficient growing space, including head height, otherwise the building could be abandoned before it has had much use. Wendy houses can be built in many different styles, but the key to success is to provide the basic fittings. Windows that open are a must, as is a roof with a chimney and some trimmings, such as curtains and child-size furniture.

LEFT: *If you have a stout tree in the garden you might think about building a treehouse. Ensure that the access and any platforms are safely built and check them often. If necessary, use extra posts for structural support and to lessen the strain on the tree branches.*

TOP RIGHT: *Happily playing in her own little world, this little girl has the perfect make-believe home. The same structure could be used to make a jungle trading post.*

RIGHT: *Robust adventure play equipment made from wood blends relatively easily into the informal garden. Specialist suppliers can provide a range of modular structures that can be fitted together, depending on the available space, including lookout towers, aerial walkways, rope climbing frames, slides and ramps. Try spray-painting the wood with a camouflage design.*

index

PICTURE CREDITS
The publishers would like to thank the following photographers for their contributions to this book:
t = top, b = bottom, l = left, r = right, c = centre
Peter Anderson p14b; **Jonathan Buckley** p41t, 46, 47b; **John Freeman** p30–31, 45; © **Jenny Hendy** p14t, 15, 16, 23, 26t, 27, 35l, 39r, 41, 43l, 56, 59l, 59r; **Simon McBride** p44; **Marie O'Hara** p12; **Debbie Patterson** p2, 10, 13, 17, 18, 25, 29b, 32, 36t, 37, 38, 47t, 49, 53l, 60, 64; **Spike Powell** p19, 22b, 52; **Graham Rae** p22t; **Jo Whitworth** p3, 4–5 Fovant Hut, Wiltshire/Christina Oates (designer), 6, 7, 8–9 Le Manoir aux Quat' Saisons, 11, 24 Hampton Court Flower Show (1999); 25b Chelsea Flower Show (1999) "Sculpture in the Garden"/George Carter (designer), 26b, 29t Hillbarn House, 33, 34, 35r, 39b, 40, 42 Fovant Hut, Wiltshire/Christina Oates (designer), 48, 50–51 Le Manoir aux Quat' Saisons, 53r, 54t, 54b, 55 Ilford Manor, Bradford-on-Avon, 58, 61; **Juliette Wade** p28, 62, 63t, 63b.